LEGAL BRIEFS

. . . .

LEGAL BRIEFS

A LAWYER'S
QUOTATION BOOK

EDITED BY
JAMES CHARLTON

McGRAW–HILL PUBLISHING COMPANY
New York St. Louis San Francisco Bogotá
Hamburg Madrid Mexico Milan Montreal
Paris São Paulo Tokyo Toronto

2 3 4 5 6 7 8 9 FGR FGR 8 9 2 1 0 9

ISBN   0-07-023972-X{PBK.}
ISBN   0-07-023971-1{H.C.}

Library of Congress Cataloging in Publication Data
Charlton, James
    Legal briefs: the lawyers quotation book / James Charlton.
        p.   cm.
    ISBN 0-07-023971-1. —ISBN 0-07-023972-x (pbk.)
    1. Law—United States—Quotations. 2. Law—Quotations.
I. Title.
KF159.C48   1989
340′ .02—dc20   89-2559
                                                         CIP

Book Design by Mary Kornblum/Hudson Studio

FOREWORD

Gathering and reading quotations on any subject is a great pleasure. Finding just the right phrase or sentiment expressed by, hopefully, a surprising author, is very satisfying. Many subjects are rich and colorful; the legal profession, in all its aspects, is an especially bountiful vein to mine. We certainly could have included four or five thousand quotations if we were of an encyclopedic mind, but instead we have culled a choice five hundred quotations on a variety of subjects near and dear to the hearts of lawyers. And yes, they do have hearts, and feelings and high standards, as I hope this book will illustrate.

As with the weather, everyone has strong opinions about lawyers, and I've tried to act as judge and include both sides of the court in this small volume. Juxtaposing quotations by learned individuals expressing opposite opinions on the same subject is gratifying to a quotemeister like myself.

Legal Briefs does not include every quote ever stated on a particular subject. There is no index of subject matter, no first lines or words, nor is there an attempt to list the source of every quotation. Even the year of the utterance or history of the author is omitted, although most names in the book will be familiar to the reader. There are many more extensive encyclopedic reference books of quotations available, including a number of quotation collections for lawyers, and these belong in every reader's library.

Legal Briefs is a small offering of quotations that amused me or touched me in some way. Many express my own sentiments, but are stated in a more eloquent manner than I ever could. I trust you will find some that amuse or provoke you as well.

Jim Charlton
New York City

LEGAL BRIEFS

. . . .

Lawyers, I suppose, were children once.
CHARLES LAMB

I learned law so well, the day I graduated I sued the college, won the case, and got my tuition back.
FRED ALLEN

In university they don't tell you that the greatest part of the law is learning to tolerate fools.
DORIS LESSING

I see nothing wrong with giving Robert some legal experience as Attorney General before he goes out to practice law.
JOHN F. KENNEDY

If law school is so hard to get through, how come there are so many lawyers?
CALVIN TRILLIN

Sometime I felt going from football to law school was quite like going from one insane asylum to another insane asylum.
MARVIN POWELL

Most good lawyers live well, work hard, and die poor.
DANIEL WEBSTER

The good lawyer is not the man who has an eye to every side and angle of contingency, and qualifies all his qualifications, but who throws himself on your part so heartily, that he can get you out of a scrape.
RALPH WALDO EMERSON

You want someone who has tasted many different situations, who struggled, who raised a family, who lived in a neighborhood all their lives rather than a penthouse on Sutton Place.

MARIO CUOMO *On Lawyers*

The profession of law is the only aristocratic element which can be amalgamated without violence with the natural elements of democracy, and which can be advantageously and permanently combined with them.

ALEXIS DE TOCQUEVILLE

No brilliance is needed in law. Nothing but common sense and relatively clean finger nails.

JOHN MORTIMER

You can't get the Monkees back together as a rock 'n roll group. That would be like Raymond Burr opening up a law practice.

MIKE NESMITH

Sometimes even lawyers need lawyers.
BILLY CARTER

A wise lawyer never goes to law himself.
PROVERB

I used to be a lawyer but now I am a reformed character.
WOODROW WILSON

Lawyer: One skilled in circumvention of the law.
Liar: A lawyer with a roving commission.
AMBROSE BIERCE

The first thing we do, let's kill all the lawyers.
WILLIAM SHAKESPEARE,
King Henry the Sixth

I think we may class lawyers in the natural history of monsters.
JOHN KEATS

Woe unto you, lawyers! For ye have taken away the key of knowledge.
ST. LUKE

The public regards lawyers with distrust. They think lawyers are smarter than the average guy, but use their intelligence deviously. Well, they're wrong. Usually they're not smarter.
F. LEE BAILEY

Sometimes a man who deserves to be looked down upon because he is a fool is despised only because he is a lawyer.
CHARLES DE SECONDAT, BARON DE MONTESQUIEU

I am not so afraid of lawyers as I used to be. They are lambs in wolves' clothing.
EDNA ST. VINCENT MILLAY

A good lawyer makes an evil neighbor.
PROVERB

A lawyer's dream of heaven — every man reclaimed his property at the resurrection, and each tried to recover it from all his forefathers.
SAMUEL BUTLER

Always remember that when you go into an attorney's office door you will have to pay for it, first or last.
ANTHONY TROLLOPE

Whenever a male client visits a lawyer, he surrenders three items in the reception room: his hat, his coat, and his manhood.
MORLEY L. TORGOV

Lawyers write badly because doing so promotes their economic interests. Every time lawyers confound their clients with a case citation, a "heretofore" or an "in the instance" case, they are letting everyone know that they possess something the nonlegal world does not.
STEVEN STARK

A man may as well open an oyster without a knife, as a lawyer's mouth without a fee.
BARTEN HOLYDAY

It was so cold one day last February that I saw a lawyer with his hands in his own pockets.
ROBERT PETERSON

God works wonders now and then;
Behold! a lawyer, an honest man.
BENJAMIN FRANKLIN

The line between a bank robber and a lawyer is a very thin one. In robbing a bank I always planned the job carefully, leaving nothing to chance. It's the same thing in trying a case. "Preparation is everything" lawyers say.
WILLIE SUTTON

Litigious terms, fat contentions, and flowing fees.
JOHN MILTON

Even the law of gravitation would be brought into dispute were there a pecuniary interest involved.
THOMAS BABINGTON MACAULAY

When there is a rift in the lute, the business of the lawyer is to widen the rift and gather the lute.
ARTHUR GARFIELD HAYS

A lawyer is a man who helps you get what's coming to him.
OSCAR LEVANT

And the more money there is, the more lawsuits there are. The bigger the artist, the more lawsuits.
JOHN LENNON

A man without money needs no more fear a crowd of lawyers than a crowd of pickpockets.
WILLIAM WYCHERLEY

The [legal] fees are outrageous. With the cost of litigation these days, I think clients would often be better off if they just met in the halls and threw dice. Certainly it would be cheaper.
WALTER MCLAUGHLIN

In the Halls of Justice the only justice is in the halls.
LENNY BRUCE

Nothing is more certain than that arguments or instructions depend on their consciousness.
ALEXANDER POPE

What do you get in place of a conscience? Don't answer. I know: a lawyer.
KIRK DOUGLAS

I don't think you can make a lawyer honest by an act of legislature. You've got to work on his conscience. And his lack of conscience is what makes him a lawyer.
WILL ROGERS

The one thing that doesn't abide by majority rule is a person's conscience.

HARPER LEE

Never do anything against conscience even if the state demands it.

ALBERT EINSTEIN

I have always proclaimed that there can be nothing finer than to be the advocate of those who cannot defend themselves.

ADOLF HITLER

I never take a case unless I am convinced my client was incapable of committing the crime charged.

PERRY MASON,
The Case of the Perjured Parrot
Erle Stanley Gardner

Bar associations are notoriously reluctant to disbar or even suspend a member unless he has murdered a judge downtown at high noon, in the presence of the entire committee on Ethical Practices.

SYDNEY J. HARRIS

A lawyer has no business with the justice or injustice of the case which he undertakes, unless his client asks his opinion, and then he is bound to give it honestly. The justice or injustice of the case is to be decided by the judge.

SAMUEL JOHNSON

Next to the confrontation between two highly trained, finely honed battery of lawyers, jungle warfare is a stately minuet.
BILL VEECK

The courtroom is a negotiating session between the State and criminal on how much the criminal must pay for having been arrested.
JERRY RUBIN

He believed in the injustice of his using any legal methods he could improvise to force the other side into compromise or into dismissals of charges, or to lead a jury into the verdict he wanted. Why not? He was a defense lawyer, not a judge or a policeman or a legislator or a theoretician or an anarchist or a murderer.
JOYCE CAROL OATES

Ninety percent of our lawyers serve ten percent of our people. We are over-lawyered and under-represented.

JIMMY CARTER

I always felt from the beginning that you had to defend people that you disliked and feared as well as those you admired.

ROGER BALDWIN

I'm a paid gladiator. I fight for my clients. Most clients aren't square shooters. That's why they're clients. They've got themselves into trouble. It's up to me to get them out. I have to shoot square with them. I can't always expect them to shoot square with me.

PERRY MASON,
The Case of the Velvet Claw
Erle Stanley Gardner

I get paid for seeing that my clients have every break the law allows. I have knowingly defended a number of guilty men. But the guilty never escape unscathed. My fees are sufficient punishment for anyone.

F. LEE BAILEY

I never was ruined but twice — once when I lost a lawsuit, and once when I gained one.

VOLTAIRE

Lawyers use the law as shoemakers use leather; rubbing it, pressing it, and stretching it with their teeth, all to the purpose of making it fit their purposes.

LOUIS XII OF FRANCE

Get them off anyway you can.
WILLIAM KUNSTLER

It's sort of an obsession with me to do the best I can for a client. My clients aren't blameless. Many of them are crooks. Probably a lot of them are guilty. That's not for me to determine. That's for a jury to determine.
PERRY MASON,
The Case of the Velvet Claw
Erle Stanley Gardner

A Lean award is better than a fat Judgement.
BENJAMIN FRANKLIN

Men keep their agreements when it is an advantage to both parties not to break them.
SOLON

A verbal contract isn't worth the paper it's written on.
SAMUEL GOLDWYN

Behind every argument is someone's ignorance. Rediscover the foundation of truth and the purpose and causes of dispute immediately disappear.
LOUIS BRANDEIS

The most savage controversies are those about matters to which there is no good evidence either way.
BERTRAND RUSSELL

How many a dispute could have been deflated into a single paragraph if the disputants had dared define their terms.
ARISTOTLE

It were endless to dispute upon everything that is disputable.

WILLIAM PENN

A difference of opinion is what makes horse racing and missionaries.

WILL ROGERS

Arguments are to be avoided. They are always vulgar and often unconvincing.

OSCAR WILDE

The worst thing you can wish someone would be: "May you be in litigation the rest of your life." I'd rather someone would kill me rather than take me to court for the rest of my life — it would be more merciful.

TOM BERENGER

Discourage litigation. Persuade your neighbor to compromise whenever you can. As a peacemaker, the lawyer has a superior opportunity of being a good man. There will still be business enough.

ABRAHAM LINCOLN

Strong and bitter words indicate a weak cause.

VICTOR HUGO

So that in the nature of man we find three principle causes of quarrel. First, competition; secondly, diffidence; thirdly, glory.

THOMAS HOBBES

In the whole history of law and order the longest step forward was taken by primitive man when, as if by common consent, the tribe sat down in a circle and allowed only one man to speak at a time. An accused who is shouted down has no rights whatsoever.

CURTIS BOK

He who establishes his argument by noise and command shows that reason is weak.

MICHEL DE MONTAIGNE

Be calm in arguing; for fierceness makes error a fault, and truth discourtesy.

GEORGE HERBERT

Opinions cannot survive if one has no chance to fight for them.

THOMAS MANN

For certain people, after fifty, litigation takes the place of sex.

GORE VIDAL

Some people think about sex all the time, some people think of sex some of the time, and some people never think about sex: they become lawyers.

WOODY ALLEN

Lawsuit, n. a machine which you go into as a pig and come out as a sausage.

AMBROSE BIERCE

An incompetent attorney can delay a trial for years or months. A competent attorney can delay one even longer.

EVELLE J. YOUNGER

It is not the bad lawyers who are screwing up the justice system in this country — it's the good lawyers. If you have two competent lawyers on opposite sides, a trial that should take three days could easily last six months.

ART BUCHWALD

Briefs for the defense are most likely to bring glory and popularity to the pleader.

MARCUS TULLIUS CICERO

There are limits to permissible misrepresentation, even at the hands of a lawyer.

JOHN MAYNARD KEYNES

All that is relied upon, in a prosecution, is an indefinable fear for other people's moral standards — a fear that I regard as a democratic anomaly.

CURTIS BOK

True opinions can prevail only if the facts to which they refer are known; if they are not known, false ideas are just as effective as true ones, if not a little more effective.

WALTER LIPPMAN

Facts are not judgements and judgements are not facts.

DICK FRANCIS

To be sure, most lawyers today recognize that their most important work is done in the office, not in the courtroom; the elaborate masked ritual of the courtroom holds attraction only for the neophyte and the layman.

DAVID REISMAN

I love confronting trial lawyers from Wall Street firms, with their pin stripe suits and doodads hanging off their shoes. We wipe the floor with them because we're trying cases all the time.

JOSEPH NAPOLI

Martial law can never exist where the courts are open, and in the proper and unobstructed exercise of their jurisdiction.

DAVID DAVIS

Whatever you do, never go to the law; submit rather to almost any imposition; bear any oppression, rather than exhaust your spirits and your pocket in what is called a court of justice.

SIR JOHN WILLES

Our courts have their faults, as does any human institution, but in this country our courts are the great levelers, and in our courts all men are created equal. I'm no idealist to believe firmly in the integrity of our courts and in our jury system — that is no ideal to me, it is a living, working reality. Gentlemen, a court is no better than each man of you sitting before me on this jury. A court is only as sound as its jury, and a jury is only as sound as the men who make it up.

HARPER LEE

In cross-examination, as in fishing, nothing is more ungainly than a fisherman pulled into the water by his catch.

LOUIS NIZER

The first rule of advocacy. Never ask your witness a question unless you're quite sure of the answer.

JOHN MORTIMER

They have been grand-jurymen since before Noah was a sailor.

WILLIAM SHAKESPEARE,
Twelfth Night

You must never explore or experiment during cross-examination. You must never ask a question if you do not already know the answer.

EDWARD BENNETT WILLIAMS

Lawyers hold that there are two kinds of particularly bad witnesses: a reluctant witness, and a too willing witness.
CHARLES DICKENS

Never, never, never, on cross-examination ask a witness a question you don't already know the answer to, was a tenet I absorbed with my baby food. Do it, and you'll often net an answer you don't want, an answer that might wreck your case.
HARPER LEE

The body is the chief witness in every murder.
G.K. CHESTERTON

Some circumstantial evidence is very strong, as when you find a trout in the milk.
HENRY DAVID THOREAU

And summed it up so well that it came to
 far more
Than the Witnesses ever had said!
LEWIS CARROLL

It appears to be taken for granted that it is a principle of American jurisprudence that men who are victims of a popular outcry are not entitled to a fair trial.
JOHN PETER ALTGELD

An appeal is when ye ask wan court to show its contempt for another court.
FINLEY PETER DUNNE

Jury: a group of twelve men who, having lied to the judge about their hearing, health, and business engagements, have failed to fool him.

H. L. MENCKEN

When you pick a good jury, the case is 90% won. I can just about look at a person and tell if I want him as a juror. If he has Gucci loafers, a Rolex watch, and a Kiwanis pin, he has his, and he has no heart for the underdog. He doesn't believe in the jury system, he doesn't like lawyers, and he's afraid of being sued. He may be the backbone of America, but he's not going to sit on my jury.

J. B. SPENCE

Th' lawyers make th' law, th' judges make th' errors, but the idiotors make th' juries.

FINLEY PETER DUNNE

A fox should not be on the jury at a goose's trial.

THOMAS FULLER

A jury consists of twelve persons chosen to decide who has a better lawyer.

ROBERT FROST

The jury, passing on the prisoner's
  life,
May in the sworn twelve have a thief or two
  Guiltier than him they try.

WILLIAM SHAKESPEARE,
All's Well That Ends Well

Since twelve honest men have
   decided the cause,
And were judges of fact, though not
   judges of laws.
   SIR WILLIAM PULTENEY

The penalty for laughing in a courtroom is six months in jail;
if it were not for this penalty, the jury would never hear the
evidence.
   H. L. MENCKEN

"I'll be judge and I'll be jury," said cunning old Fury;
"I'll try the whole cause and condemn you to death."
   LEWIS CARROLL

The public can't tell good writing when they see it, and neither can plenty of editors and publishers. Still, the good writers become popular. I guess they succeed for the same reason that the jury system succeeds.
  RED SMITH

Trial by jury itself, instead of being a security to persons who are accused, will be a delusion, a mockery, and a snare.
  LORD DENMAN

The hungry judges soon the sentence sign,
And wretches hang that jurymen may dine.
  ALEXANDER POPE

Jury service honestly performed is as important in the defense of our country, its Constitution and laws, and the ideals and standards for which they stand, as the service that is rendered by the soldier on the field of battle in the time of war.

GEORGE H. BOLDT

"No! No!" said the Queen, "Sentence first — verdict afterwards."

LEWIS CARROLL

I don't want to know what the law is, I want to know who the judge is.

ROY COHN

I may not know much about law, but I do know one can put the fear of God into judges.

THEODORE ROOSEVELT

Now, the law is good but some of these judges just don't know how to handle it in court. They simply don't have the experience. There are an awful lot of "C" law students practising law and sitting on the bench.

MELVIN BELLI

I am as sober as a judge.

HENRY FIELDING

Judge — A law student who marks his own examination papers.

H.L. MENCKEN

Judges are best in the beginning; they deteriorate as time passes.
CORNELIUS TACITUS

That judges of important causes should hold office for life is not a good thing, for the mind grows old as well as the body.
ARISTOTLE

Decisions of the judges will be final unless shouted down by an overwhelming majority of the fans.
Addenda to the rules of the first International Boomerang Tournamant

Judges, so long as they are relatively normal human beings, can no more escape public opinion in the long run than can people working at other jobs.
WILLIAM REHNQUIST

Judges should not be influenced by the weather of the day, but they should be influenced by the climate of the age.
PAUL A. FREUND

Nothing is more difficult, and therefore more precious, than being able to decide.
NAPOLEON BONAPARTE

The most terrible thing is your own judgment.
ROBERT FROST

The foolish and the dead alone never change their opinions.
JAMES RUSSELL LOWELL

There are only two ways to be quite unprejudiced and impartial. One is to be completely ignorant. The other is to be completely indifferent. Bias and prejudice are attitudes to be kept in hand, not attitudes to be avoided.
CHARLES P. CURTIS

Nobody has a more sacred obligation to obey the law than those who make the law.
JEAN ANOUILH

The two great evils in the execution of our criminal laws today are sentimentality and technicality.
THEODORE ROOSEVELT

I have been mad with work. First, a stinker of a case that frightened me, and then, as 500 times before, gradually sank to the dimensions of a poodle, no longer diabolic except for the longwindedness and confused argument of counsel.
OLIVER WENDELL HOLMES, JR.

The presence of one of our regular civilian judge-advocates in an army in the field would be a first-class nuisance.
WILLIAM T. SHERMAN

Laws are a dead letter without courts to expound and define their true meaning and operation.
ALEXANDER HAMILTON

When I talk of law I talk as a cynic. I don't care a damn if twenty professors tell me that a decision is not law if I know that the courts will enforce it.
OLIVER WENDELL HOLMES, JR.

Wilson Mizner, a gambler, wit and playwright, was brought into a courtroom on some charge or other. During the proceedings, the judge said angrily, "Are you trying to show contempt of court?" To which Mizner replied, "No, your Honor, I am trying to conceal it."

IRVING WALLACE

Young lawyers attend the courts, not because they have business there, but because they have business nowhere else.

WASHINGTON IRVING

This is a court of law, young man, not a court of justice.

OLIVER WENDELL HOLMES, JR.

It is better that a judge should lean on the side of compassion than severity.

MIGUEL DE CERVANTES

The judge who does not agonize before passing a sentence is a criminal.

JOHN CIARDI

If you can take upon yourself the crime of the criminal your heart is judging, take it at once, suffer for him yourself, and let him go without reproach. And even if the law itself makes you his judge, act in the same spirit, so far as possible, for he will go away and condemn himself more bitterly than you have done.

FYODOR DOSTOYEVSKY

It is better to risk saving a guilty person than to condemn an innocent one.

VOLTAIRE

It is better that ten guilty persons than one innocent suffer.
SIR WILLIAM BLACKSTONE

The confession of evil works is the first beginning of good works.
ST. AUGUSTINE

We have to choose, and for my part I think it a less evil that some criminals should escape than that the government should play an ignoble part.
OLIVER WENDELL HOLMES, JR.

Crimes are not to be measured by the issue of events but from the bad intentions of men.
MARCUS TULLIUS CICERO

Little crimes lead to big crimes.
DICK TRACY
Chester Gould

Few men have virtue to withstand the highest bidder.
GEORGE WASHINGTON

Alas! the small discredit of a bribe
Scarce hurts the lawyer, but undoes the scribe.
ALEXANDER POPE

The accomplice to the crime of corruption is frequently our own indifference.
BESS MYERSON

There is no den in the whole world to hide a rogue. Commit a crime and the earth is made of glass. Commit a crime, and it seems as if a coat of snow fell on the ground, such as reveals in the woods the track of every partridge, and fox, and squirrel.
RALPH WALDO EMERSON

The law's made to take care o' raskills.
GEORGE ELIOT

Criminal law is the only profession in which the better you get, the worse the class of people you represent.
EDWARD HAYES

A barrister's profession is such an uncertain thing, especially if he won't undertake unsavory cases.
HENRIK IBSEN

It is a fair summary of history to say that the safeguards of liberty have frequently been forged in cases involving not very nice people.
FELIX FRANKFURTER

You can't earn a living defending innocent people.
MAURICE NADJARI

If there were no bad people, there would be no good lawyers.
CHARLES DICKENS

The cheaper the crook, the gaudier the patter.
SAM SPADE,
The Maltese Falcon
Dashiell Hammett

Organized crime is a blight on our nation. While many young Americans are lured into a career of crime by its promise of an easy life, most criminals must work long hours, frequently in buildings without air conditioning.
WOODY ALLEN

Successful and fortunate crime is called virtue.
SENECA

We easily forget crimes that are known only to ourselves.
FRANCOIS DUKE DE LA ROCHEFOUCAULD

But many a crime, deem's innocent
   on earth,
Is registered in Heaven; and these,
   no doubt,
Have each their record, with a curse
   annex'd.
   WILLIAM COWPER

The criminal is the creative artist; the detective only the critic.
   G. K. CHESTERTON

Life is nothing but a competition to be the criminal rather than the victim.
   BERTRAND RUSSELL

People like killers. And if one feels sympathy for the victims it's by way of thanking them for letting themselves be killed.
   EUGENE IONESCO

Murderers, in general, are people who are consistent, people who are obsessed with one idea and nothing else. And that applies to their victims, as well.
   UGO BETTI

Everybody is a potential murderer. I've never killed anybody, but I frequently get satisfaction reading the obituary section.
   CLARENCE DARROW

No crime can be successful without luck!
   HERCULE POIROT,
   The A.B.C. Murders
   Agatha Christie

Nobody ever commits a crime without doing something stupid.

OSCAR WILDE

The contempt for law and the contempt for the human consequences of lawbreaking go from the bottom to the top of American society.

MARGARET MEAD

I think it is morally wrong for the murderer to survive the victim at taxpayer's expense.

ERNEST VAN DEN HAAG

If Robert Kennedy were alive today he would not countenance singling me out for this kind of treatment.

SIRHAN SIRHAN, *arguing in front of his parole board*

I have too great a soul to die like a criminal.

JOHN WILKES BOOTH

Stupid men — you who believe in laws which punish murder by murder and who express vengeance in calumny and defamation.

GEORGE SAND

The long and distressing controversy over capital punishment is very unfair to anyone contemplating murder.

GEOFFREY FISHER

The reformative effect of punishment is a belief that dies hard, chiefly, I think, because it is so satisfying to our sadistic impulse.

BERTRAND RUSSELL

Capital punishment is as fundamentally wrong as a cure for crime as charity is wrong as a cure for poverty.
HENRY FORD

Distrust all in whom the impulse to punish is powerful.
FREDERICH NIETZSCHE

Punishment brings wisdom; it is the healing art of wickedness.
PLATO

Speaking generally, punishment hardens and numbs, it produces concentration, it sharpens the consciousness of alienation, it strengthens the power of resistance.
FREDERICH NIETZSCHE

When a man knows he is to be hanged in a fortnight, it concentrates his mind wonderfully.
SAMUEL JOHNSON

No man has ever yet been hanged for breaking the spirit of a law.
GROVER CLEVELAND

Men are not hanged for stealing horses but that horses may not be stolen.
LORD HALIFAX

The contagion of crime is like that of the plague. Criminals collected together corrupt each other. They are worse than ever when, at the termination of their punishment, they return to society.
NAPOLEON BONAPARTE

When bad men combine, the good must associate; else they will fall one by one.

EDMUND BURKE

With ready-made opinions one cannot judge of crime. Its philosophy is a little more complicated than people think. It is acknowledged that neither convict prisons, nor the hulks, nor any system of hard labor ever cured a criminal.

FYODOR DOSTOYEVSKY

Identifying criminals is up to each of us. Usually they can be recognized by their large cufflinks and their failure to stop eating when the man next to them is hit by a falling anvil.

WOODY ALLEN

Chemists employed by the police can do remarkable things with blood. They can find it in shreds of cloth, in the interstices of floor boards, on the iron of a heel, and can measure it and swear to it and weave it into a rope to hang a man.

MARGERY ALLINGHAM

If poverty is the mother of crime, want of sense is the father of them.

JEAN DE LA BRUYERE

Crimes sometimes shock us too much; vices almost always too little.

A. W. AND J. C. CLARKE

Reason to rule, but mercy to forgive:
The first is law, the last prerogative.

JOHN DRYDEN

Mercy is not what every criminal is entitled to. What he is entitled to is justice.

LORD HAILSHAM

For many persons, law appears to be black magic — an obscure domain that can be fathomed only by the professional initiated into its mysteries.

SUSAN C. ROSS

The laws I love, the lawyers I suspect.

CHARLES CHURCHILL

If the laws could speak for themselves they would complain of the lawyers in the first place.

LORD HALIFAX

The term "Rule of Law," like the phrase "Love of God" and "Brotherhood of Man," is a short and simple expression of one of the few most sublime concepts that the mind and spirit of man has yet achieved.

GEORGE H. BOLDT

Laws and institutions must go hand in hand with the progress of the human mind.

THOMAS JEFFERSON

Sir Thomas More: The law, Roper, the law. I know what's legal and what's right. And I'll stick to what's legal.
Roper: So now you'd give the Devil benefit of law!
Sir Thomas: Yes. What would you do? Cut a great road through the law to get after the Devil?
Roper: I'd cut down every law in England to do that!
Sir Thomas: Oh? And when the last law was down and the Devil turned round on you where would you hide, Roper, the laws all being flat?

ROBERT BOLT

The safety of the people shall be the highest law.

MARCUS TULLIUS CICERO

No man is above the law and no man is below it: nor do we ask any man's permission when we ask him to obey it.

THEODORE ROOSEVELT

Man became free when he recognized that he was subject to law.

WILL DURANT

Fragile as reason is and limited as law is as the institution-alized medium of reason, that's all we have standing between us and the tyranny of mere will and the cruelty of unbridled, undisciplined feeling.

FELIX FRANKFURTER

The law is reason free from passion.

ARISTOTLE

Law is the mechanism of human affairs.

SUN YAT-SEN

Law is intelligence, whose natural function it is to command right conduct and forbid wrongdoing.

MARCUS TULLIUS CICERO

The law is the last result of human wisdom acting upon human experience for the benefit of the public.

SAMUEL JOHNSON

The Law is the true embodiment
Of everything that's excellent.
It has not kind of fault or flaw,
And I, my Lords, embody the Law.

SIR W. S. GILBERT

The law is not an end in itself, nor does it provide ends. It is preeminently a means to serve what we think is right.

WILLIAM J. BRENNAN

The law is good, if a man use it lawfully.

ST. TIMOTHY

The law is nature. The law is only a word for what has a right to happen.

ARTHUR MILLER

The laws of God, the laws of man,
He may keep that will and can;
Not I: let god and man decree
Laws for themselves and not for me.

A. E. HOUSMAN

We are always saying let the law take its course, but what we mean is "Let the law take our course."

WILL ROGERS

There is. . .but one categorical imperative: Act only on that maxim whereby thou canst at the time will that it should become universal law.

IMMANUEL KANT

The laws keep up their credit, not by being just, but because they are laws; 'tis the mystic foundation of their authority.

MICHEL DE MONTAIGNE

The law: It has honored us; may we honor it.

DANIEL WEBSTER

The aim of law is the maximum gratification of the nervous system of man.

LEARNED HAND

Laws are never as effective as habits.

ADLAI STEVENSON

There are two restrictions on human liberty — the restraint of law and that of custom. No written law has ever been more binding than unwritten custom supported by popular opinion.

CARRIE CHAPMAN CATT

Laws describe constraint. Their purpose is to control, not to create.

TOM ROBBINS

We, like the eagles, were born to be free. Yet we are obliged, in order to live at all, to make a cage of laws for ourselves and to stand on the perch.

WILLIAM BOLITHO

Power gradually extirpates from the mind every humane and gentle virtue.
EDMUND BURKE

Every law is an infraction of liberty.
JEREMY BENTHAM

As soon as laws are necessary for men, they are no longer fit for freedom.
PYTHAGORAS

I think you have to have laws to live by. If you're plowing a mule out there, I don't think you can jump ahead of the mule. You gotta stay behind the dad-gummed plow.
JERRY LEE LEWIS

Few laws are of universal application. It is the nature of our law that it has dealt not with man in general, but with him in relationships.
LOUIS BRANDEIS

No great idea in its beginning can ever be within the law. How can it be within the law? The law is stationary. The law is fixed. The law is a chariot wheel which binds us all regardless of conditions or place or time.
EMMA GOLDMAN

Law is merely the expression of the will of the strongest for the time being, and therefore laws have no fixity, but shift from generation to generation.
> HENRY BROOKS ADAMS

The law must be stable and yet must not stand still.
> ROSCOE POUND

Every new time will give its law.
> MAXIM GORKY

Public opinion is always in advance of the law.
> JOHN GALSWORTHY

It usually takes a hundred years to make a law; and then, after it has done its work, it usually takes a hundred years to get rid of it.
> HENRY WARD BEECHER

Laws are inherited like diseases.
> JOHANN WOLFGANG VON GOETHE

After all, that is what laws are for, to be made and unmade.
> EMMA GOLDMAN

Laws are not masters but servants, and he rules them who obeys them.
> HENRY WARD BEECHER

We are in bondage to the law in order that we may be free.
> MARCUS TULLIUS CICERO

Laws do not persuade just because they threaten.
> SENECA

There's a lot of law at the end of a nightstick.
GROVER WHALEN,
NYC Police Commissioner, 1928–1930

If law is not made more than a policeman's nightstick, American society will be destroyed.
ARTHUR GOLDBERG

The laws are silent in the midst of arms.
MARCUS TULLIUS CICERO

Useless laws weaken the necessary laws.
CHARLES DE SECONDAT, BARON DE MONTESQUIEU

Law is mighty, necessity is mightier.
JOHANN WOLFGANG VON GOETHE

A law is not a law without coercion behind it.
JAMES A. GARFIELD

Law is whatever is boldly asserted and plausibly maintained.
AARON BURR

Those who are too lazy and comfortable to think for themselves and be their own judges obey the laws. Others sense their own laws within them.
HERMAN HESSE

One with the law is a majority.
CALVIN COOLIDGE

Law is a bottomless pit.
JOHN ARBUTHNOT

Law is a bottomless pit; it is a cormorant, a harpy that devours everything.

JONATHAN SWIFT

Make laws as though all men were good: The wicked triumph, the good are crushed.

Make laws as though all men were evil: The wicked slip through them or circumvent them. Only the good obey them and suffer.

COUNT MAURICE MAETERLINCK

Laws are the product of selfishness, deception, and party prejudice. True justice is not in them, and cannot be in them.

LEO TOLSTOY

The state of nature has a law of nature to govern it, which obliges everyone; and reason, which is that law, teaches all mankind who will but consult it, that, being all equal and independent, no one ought to harm another in his life, health, liberty, or possessions.

JOHN LOCKE

How long soever it hath continued, if it be against reason it is of no force in law.

SIR EDWARD COKE

Every so often, we pass laws repealing human nature.

HOWARD LINDSAY AND RUSSEL CROUSE

Against human nature one cannot legislate. One can only try to educate it, and that is a slow process with only a distant hope of success.

BERNARD BERENSON

No laws are binding on the human subject which assault the body or violate the human spirit.

SIR WILLIAM BLACKSTONE

Every law which originated in ignorance and malice, and gratifies the passions from which it sprang, we call the wisdom of our ancestors.

SYDNEY SMITH

The Common Law of England has been laboriously built up about a very mythical figure — the figure of 'the reasonable man.'

SIR ALAN P. HERBERT

The life of the law has not been logic, it has been experience.

OLIVER WENDELL HOLMES, JR.

Mastering the lawless science of our
  law,
That codeless myriad of precedent,
That wilderness of single instances.
    ALFRED LORD TENNYSON

Mere precedent is a dangerous source of authority.
    ANDREW JACKSON

All bad precedents began as justifiable measures.
    JULIUS CAESAR

Don't use the conduct of a fool as a precedent.
    TALMUD

Legal precedents are like statistics. If you manipulate them,
you can prove anything.
    ARTHUR HAILEY

Statistics are no substitute for judgement.
    HENRY CLAY

A lawyer without history or literature is a mechanic, a mere
working mason; if he possesses some knowledge of these,
he may venture to call himself an architect.
    SIR WALTER SCOTT

The history of the Supreme Court is not the history of an
abstraction, but the analysis of individuals acting as a Court
who make decisions and lay down doctrine, and of other
individuals, their successors, who refine, modify, and
sometimes even overrule the decisions of their predecessors, reinterpreting and transmuting their doctrines.
    FELIX FRANKFURTER

The law hath not been dead, though it hath slept.

WILLIAM SHAKESPEARE,
Measure for Measure

Law cannot stand aside from the social changes around it.

WILLIAM J. BRENNAN

It doesn't do good to open doors for someone who doesn't have the price to get in. If he has the price, he may not need the laws. There is no law saying the Negro has to live in Harlem or Watts.

RONALD REAGAN

The law is bigger than money — if only the law works hard enough.

THOMAS E. DEWEY

Morality cannot be legislated but behavior can be regulated. Judicial decrees may not change the heart, but they can restrain the heartless.

MARTIN LUTHER KING, JR.

The highest virtue is always against the law.

RALPH WALDO EMERSON

If by mere force of numbers a majority should deprive a minority of any clearly written constitutional right I might, in a moral point of view, justify revolution — certainly would if such a right were a vital one.

ABRAHAM LINCOLN

If every man and woman and child in the world had a chance to make a decent, fair, honest living, there would be no jails, and no lawyers and no courts.

CLARENCE DARROW

In spite of all the cynics say, the infallible way of inducing a sense of wrongdoing is by making laws.

WILLIAM BOLITHO

"If the law supposes that," said Mr. Bumble..."the law is an ass...an idiot."

CHARLES DICKENS,
Oliver Twist

Our laws make law impossible; our liberties destroy all freedom; our property is organized robbery; our morality an impudent hypocrisy; our wisdom is administered by inexperienced or mal-experienced dupes; our power wielded by cowards and weaklings; and our honour false in all its points. I am an enemy of the existing order for good reasons.

GEORGE BERNARD SHAW

Good men must not obey the laws too well.

RALPH WALDO EMERSON

The best laws should be constructed as to leave as little as possible decision to the judge.

ARISTOTLE

There will be more flexibility about the legal system in the Almost Perfect State than there is in our own legal system. There will be, of course, a great many laws, but no person will be expected to obey a law that someone else has made if he himself can make a law on the spur of the moment that is a better law and more justly applicable to his own case.

DON MARQUIS

They have no lawyers among them, for they consider them as a sort of people whose profession it is to disguise matters.

SIR THOMAS MORE

Ignorance of the law excuses no man; not that all men know the law, but because 'tis an excuse every man will plead, and no man can tell how to refute him.

JOHN SELDEN

The laws which apply to most of us cannot be rationally applied to professional sports.

DICK YOUNG

It simply wouldn't be possible to establish rules which could be applied fairly and reasonably to sports in general. Anyone who tries to deal authoritatively with the particular and individual problems of sport would have to have the knowledge of the Almighty, the judgement of Solomon and the vision of Joan of Arc. I don't find those qualities available in anyone, not even Howard Cosell.

PETE ROZELLE

These days it's not as important to know the difference between a veer offense and a wishbone as to know the difference between a preliminary hearing and a temporary injunction.

BOB WOOLF

The law has no power to command obedience except that of habit, which can only be given by time, so that a readiness to change from old to new laws enfeebles the power of the law.

ARISTOTLE

Laws and institutions are constantly tending to gravitate. Like clocks, they must be occasionally cleansed, and wound up, and set to true time.

HENRY WARD BEECHER

Good laws lead to the making of better ones; bad ones bring about worse.

JEAN JACQUES ROUSSEAU

Bad laws are the worst sort of tyranny.

EDMUND BURKE

Hard cases, it is said, make bad law.

LORD JOHN CAMPBELL

Great cases, like hard cases, make bad law.

OLIVER WENDELL HOLMES, JR.

To be sure judicial doctrine is one thing, practice another. The pressure of so-called great cases is something too much for judicial self-restraint, and the Supreme Court from time to time in its history has forgotten its own doctrines when they should have remembered most.

FELIX FRANKFURTER

Laws were made to be broken.
CHRISTOPHER NORTH

Unjust laws exist: Shall we be content to obey them, or shall we endeavor to amend them, and obey them until we have succeeded, or shall we transgress them at once?
HENRY DAVID THOREAU

Nothing is more destructive of respect for the government and the law of the land then passing laws which cannot be enforced.
ALBERT EINSTEIN

In a number of cases dissenting opinions have in time become the law.
CHARLES EVANS HUGHES

Even when laws have been written down, they ought not always to remain unaltered.
ARISTOTLE

Laws too gentle are seldom obeyed; too severe, seldom executed.
BENJAMIN FRANKLIN

Law and justice are not always the same. When they aren't, destroying the law may be the first step toward changing it.
GLORIA STEINEM

The execution of the laws is more important than making them.
THOMAS JEFFERSON

I know of no method to secure the repeal of bad or obnoxious law so effective as their stringent execution.

ULYSSES S. GRANT

When laws cease to have usefulness to society, they should be changed, not enforced. All one has to do is to think of the jimcrow laws of most states in the South not so many years ago to know what I mean.

CORETTA SCOTT KING

Necessity hath no law.

OLIVER CROMWELL

Legem non habet necessitas. (Necessity knows no law.)

ST. AUGUSTINE

When men are pure, laws are useless; when men are corrupt, laws are broken.

BENJAMIN DISRAELI

Probably all laws are useless; for good men do not want laws at all, and bad men are made no better by them.

DEMONAX OF CYPRUS

The language of the law must not be foreign to the ears of those who are to obey it.

LEARNED HAND

The minute you read something you can't understand, you can almost be sure it was drawn up by a lawyer.

WILL ROGERS

There are two things wrong with almost all legal writing. One is style. The other is content.

FRED RODELL

The training of lawyers is a training in logic. The processes of analogy, discrimination, and deduction are those in which they are most at home. The language of judicial decision is mainly the language of logic. And the logical method and form flatter that longing for certainty and for repose which is in every human mind. But certainty generally is illusion, and repose is not the destiny of man.

OLIVER WENDELL HOLMES, JR.

In legal briefs or opinions almost all footnotes are unnecessary. Avoid them assiduously.

WILLIAM BABLITCH

Some lawyers may fear some of their mystique will be gone if they don't use five-syllable words.

DONALD C. SCHILLER

Written laws are like spider's webs, and will like them only entangle and hold the poor and weak, while the rich and powerful will easily break through them.

ANACHARSIS

People starting with the idea that certain things are right and are the law, come to believe that others are right because they are the law.

W. SOMERSET MAUGHAM

When you have robbed a man of everything, he is no longer in your power. He is free again.

ALEKSANDR SOLZHENITSYN

People, crushed by law, have no hopes but power.

EDMUND BURKE

The law, unfortunately, has always been retained on the side of power; laws have uniformly been enacted for the perpetuation of power.

THOMAS COOPER

Law? What do I need with the law? Hain't I got the power?

CORNELIUS VANDERBILT

Power is not sufficient evidence of truth.

SAMUEL JOHNSON

The truth is that all men having power ought to be mistrusted.

JAMES MADISON

Gentlemen:
You have undertaken to cheat me.
I will not sue you, for law takes too
long. I will ruin you.
Sincerely yours,

CORNELIUS VANDERBILT

A man's respect for law and order exists in precise relationship to the size of his paycheck.

ADAM CLAYTON POWELL

I don't want a lawyer to tell me what I cannot do; I hire him to tell me how to do what I want to do.

J. P. MORGAN

It is not what a lawyer tells me I may do; but what humanity, reason, and justice tell me I ought to do.

EDMUND BURKE

Law is but a heathen word for power.
DANIEL DEFOE

Where public opinion is free and uncontrolled, wealth has a wholesome respect for law.
ROBERT M. LAFOLLETTE, SR.

Laws grind the poor, and rich men rule the Law.
OLIVER GOLDSMITH

Nobody is poor unless he stands in need of justice.
LACTANTIUS

There are no eternal facts, as there are no absolute truths.
FRIEDRICH NIETZSCHE

If the poor man is not able to support his suit according to the vexations and expensive manner established in civilized countries, has not the rich as great an advantage over him as the strong has over the weak in a state of nature?
EDMUND BURKE

People say law but they mean wealth.
RALPH WALDO EMERSON

Law is where you buy it in this town.
PHILLIP MARLOWE,
Farewell My Lovely
Raymond Chandler

The law, in its majestic equality, forbids the rich as well as the poor to sleep under bridges, to beg in the streets, and to steal bread.
ANATOLE FRANCE

Everyone has as much right as he might.
BENEDICT SPINOZA

Let us have faith that right makes might; and in that faith let us to the end, dare to do our duty as we understand it.
ABRAHAM LINCOLN

Success is the sole earthly judge of right and wrong.
ADOLF HITLER

What is right and what is practicable are two different things.
JAMES BUCHANAN

Writs of assistance and general warrants are but puny instruments of tyranny compared to wiretapping.
LOUIS BRANDEIS

Law enforcement, however, in defeating the criminal, must maintain inviolate the historic liberties of the individual.
J. EDGAR HOOVER

If at the bottom of law and order there is only a man armed to the teeth, a man without a heart, without a conscience, then law and order are meaningless.
HENRY MILLER

A man may not accuse himself of a crime.
TALMUD

Never sue for assault or slander, settle them cases yourself.
ANDREW JACKSON

The greater the truth the greater the libel.
EDWARD LAW

It takes your enemy and your friend, working together to hurt you to the heart; the one to slander you and the other to get the news to you.
MARK TWAIN

Libelous: To be tactless in type.
FRANK MCKINNEY HUBBARD

He that flings dirt at another dirtieth himself most.
THOMAS FULLER

A man's reputation is not in his own keeping, but lies at the mercy of the profligacy of others. Calumny requires no proof. The throwing out of malicious imputations against any character leaves a stain, which no after refutation can wipe out. To create an unfavorable impression, it is not necessary that certain things should be true, but that they have been said. The imagination is of so delicate a texture that even words wound it.

WILLIAM HAZLITT

No real gentleman would tell the truth in the presence of ladies.

MARK TWAIN

It is hard to believe that a man is telling the truth when you know that you would lie if you were in his place.

H.L. MENCKEN

If you have reason to suspect that a person is telling you a lie, look as though you believed every word he said. This will give him the courage to go on; he will become more vehement in his assertions, and in the end betray himself.

ARTHUR SCHOPENHAUER

Lying is forbidden, even to the detection of heretics.

ST. AUGUSTINE

The General Rule is that truth should never be violated; there must however be some exceptions. If, for instance, a murderer should ask you which way a man has gone.

SAMUEL JOHNSON

I do not mind lying, but I hate inaccuracy.
SAMUEL BUTLER

Still you keep o' the windy side of law.
WILLIAM SHAKESPEARE,
Twelfth Night

Men of most reknowned virtue have sometimes by trans-
gressing most truly kept the law.
JOHN MILTON

See everything: overlook a great deal: correct a little.
POPE JOHN XXIII

A little inaccuracy sometimes saves tons of explanation.
SAKI

We want the facts to fit the preconceptions. When they don't, it is easier to ignore the facts than to change the preconceptions.

JESSAMYN WEST

There are no facts, only interpretations.

FREDERICH NIETZSCHE

Logic is neither an art nor a science, but a dodge.

STENDHAL

Immutable principles must accommodate themselves to facts of life, for facts are stubborn and will not yield. In truth, what are now deemed immutable principles once, themselves, grew out of living conditions.

FELIX FRANKFURTER

There is nothing more horrible than the murder of a beautiful theory by a brutal gang of facts.

FRANCOIS DUKE DE LA ROCHEFOUCAULD

Facts do not cease to exist because they are ignored.

ALDOUS HUXLEY

To some lawyers, all facts are created equal.

FELIX FRANKFURTER

A little fact will sustain a lot of illusion.

ERIC AMBLER

To do a great right, do a little wrong.

WILLIAM SHAKESPEARE,
Merchant of Venice

There is no better way of exercising the imagination than the study of law. No poet ever interpreted nature as freely as a lawyer interprets truth.

JEAN GIRAUDOUX

There is nothing so powerful as truth, and often nothing so strange.

DANIEL WEBSTER

How often have I said to you that when you have eliminated the impossible, whatever remains, however, improbable, must be the truth?

SHERLOCK HOLMES,
Sir Arthur Conan Doyle

Lawyers enjoy a little mystery you know. Why, if everybody came forward and told the truth, the whole truth, and nothing but the truth straight out, we should all retire to the workhouse.

DOROTHY SAYERS

Whatever is only almost true is quite false, and among the most dangerous of errors, because being so near truth, it is the more likely to lead astray.

HENRY WARD BEECHER

A truth that's told with bad intent
Beats all lies you can invent.

WILLIAM BLAKE

Veracity does not consist in saying, but in the intention of communicating truth.

WILLIAM COLERIDGE

Follow not truth too near the heels, lest it dash out thy teeth.
GEORGE HERBERT

Love truth, but pardon error.
VOLTAIRE

Truth never damages a cause that is just.
MAHATMA GANDHI

Risk! Risk anything! Care no more for the opinion of others, for those voices. Do the hardest thing on earth for you. Act for yourself. Face the truth.
KATHERINE MANSFIELD

I speak the truth, not so much as I would, but as much as I dare; and I dare a little more as I grow older.
MICHEL DE MONTAIGNE

If you tell the truth you don't have to remember anything.
MARK TWAIN

It makes all the difference in the world whether one puts truth in the first place or in the second.
WILLIAM COLERIDGE

Eternal truths will be neither true nor eternal unless they have fresh meaning for every new social situation.
FRANKLIN D. ROOSEVELT

There are truths which are not for all men, nor for all times.
VOLTAIRE

Truth has a way of shifting under pressure.
CURTIS BOK

Whatever comes to pass, comes to pass according to laws
and rules which involve eternal necessity and truth.

BENEDICT SPINOZA

If we say truth, we also say freedom and justice; if we speak
of freedom and justice, we mean truth.

THOMAS MANN

It is a fine thing to face machine guns for immortality and a
medal, but isn't it a fine thing, too, to face calumny, injustice
and loneliness for the truth which makes men free?

H. L. MENCKEN

The man who fears no truths has nothing to fear from lies.

THOMAS JEFFERSON

Truth is such a precious article let us all economize in its use.

MARK TWAIN

Great is truth. Fire cannot burn, nor water drown it.

ALEXANDRE DUMAS

Truth forever on a scaffold,
Wrong forever on a throne.

JAMES RUSSELL LOWELL

Truth is mysterious, elusive, ever to be won anew. Liberty is
dangerous, as hard to get along with as it is exciting.

ALBERT CAMUS

Truth and sincerity have a certain distinguishing native
luster about them which cannot be perfectly counterfeited;
they are like fire and flame, that cannot be painted.

BENJAMIN FRANKLIN

Those who are themselves incapable of great crimes, are ever backward to suspect others.

FRANCOIS DUKE DE LA ROCHEFOUCAULD

There is one way to find out if a man is honest — ask him. If he says "yes," you know he is crooked.

GROUCHO MARX

To believe all men honest would be folly.
To believe none so, is something worse.

JOHN QUINCY ADAMS

And whether you're an honest man, or whether you're a thief,
Depends on whose solicitor has given me my brief.

SIR W. S. GILBERT

What use is an honest lawyer when what you need is a dishonest one?

ERIC AMBLER

Whenever men take the law into their own hands, the loser is the law. And when law loses, freedom languishes.

ROBERT KENNEDY

Every dictator is an enemy of freedom, an opponent of law.

DEMOSTHENES

Where law ends, tyranny begins.

WILLIAM PITT

Liberty is the right to do whatever the laws permit.

CHARLES DE SECONDAT, BARON DE MONTESQUIEU

When dictators and tyrants seek to destroy the freedoms of men, their first target is the legal profession and through it the rule of law.

LEON JAWORSKI

Liberty means responsibility. That is why most men dread it.

GEORGE BERNARD SHAW

Too little liberty brings stagnation, and too much brings chaos.

BERTRAND RUSSELL

It is the duty of the liberal to protect and to extend the basic democratic freedom.

CHESTER BOWLES

Liberty does not consist in mere declarations of the rights of man. It consists in the translation of those declarations into definite action.

WOODROW WILSON

People hardly ever make use of the freedom they have, for example, freedom of thought; instead they demand freedom of speech as compensation.

SOREN KIERKEGAARD

People do not understand liberty or majorities. The will of a majority is the will of a rabble. Progressive democracy is incompatible with liberty.

JOHN C. CALHOUN

You can only protect your liberties in this world by protecting the other man's freedom. You can only be free if I am free.
CLARENCE DARROW

The right to work, I had assumed, was the most precious liberty that man possesses. Man has indeed as much right to work as he has to live, to be free, to own property.
WILLIAM O. DOUGLAS

The liberty of the individual to do as he pleases, even in innocent matters, is not absolute. It must frequently yield to the common good.
GEORGE SUTHERLAND

The right to be let alone is indeed the beginning of all freedom.
WILLIAM O. DOUGLAS

Equality is the result of human organization. We are not born equal.
HANNAH ARENDT

The fight must go on. The cause of civil liberty must not be surrendered at the end of one or even one hundred defeats.
ABRAHAM LINCOLN

The law regards man as man and takes no account of his surroundings or of his color when his civil rights as guaranteed by the supreme law of the land are involved.
JOHN MARSHALL HARLAN

We have confused the free with the free and easy.
ADLAI STEVENSON

Liberty is not just an idea, an abstract principle. It is power, effective power to do specific things. There is no such thing as liberty in general, liberty, so to speak, at large.

JOHN DEWEY

I believe that every right implies a responsibility; every opportunity, an obligation; every possession, a duty.

JOHN D. ROCKEFELLER, JR.

To renounce liberty is to renounce being a man, to surrender the rights of humanity and even its duties.

JEAN JACQUES ROUSSEAU

We hold that obscenity is not within the area of constitutionally protected speech or press.

WILLIAM J. BRENNAN

The liberty of thinking and publishing whatsoever each one likes, without any hindrance, is not in itself an advantage over which society can wisely rejoice. On the contrary, it is the fountainhead and origin of many evils.

POPE LEO XIII

It is, however, an evil for which there is no remedy, our liberty depends on the freedom of the press, and that cannot be limited without being lost.

THOMAS JEFFERSON

Freedom to publish means freedom for all and not for some. Freedom to publish is guaranteed by the Constitution, but freedom to continue to prevent others from publishing is not.

HUGO L. BLACK

Restriction of free thought and free speech is the most dangerous of all subversions. It is the one un-American act that could easily defeat us.

WILLIAM O. DOUGLAS

The right to be heard does not automatically include the right to be taken seriously.

HENRIK IBSEN

The right is more precious than peace.

WOODROW WILSON

Is the relinquishment of trial by jury and the liberty of the press necessary for your liberty? Will the abandonment of your most sacred rights tend to anyone's security? Liberty, the greatest of all earthly blessings give us that precious jewel and you may take everything else. . .Suspect everyone who approaches that jewel.

PATRICK HENRY

Equity is the outcome of facts, law is the application of principles to facts.

HONORE DE BALZAC

Equity speaks softly and wins in the end. But it is expedience, with its loud voice, that sets the time of victory.

CAROLINE BIRD

The reason why the Goddess is blindfolded is so she cannot see what the lawyers and judges do.

FRANK MCKINNEY HUBBARD

The law is not the private property of lawyers, nor is justice the exclusive province of judges and juries.
    JIMMY CARTER

Justice, sir, is the great interest of man on earth.
    DANIEL WEBSTER

The love of justice is, in the majority of men, the fear of suffering injustice.
    FRANCOIS DUKE DE LA ROCHEFOUCAULD

Why should there not be a patient confidence in the ultimate justice of the people? Is there any better or equal hope in the world?

ABRAHAM LINCOLN

Justice is too good for some people, and not good enough for the rest.

NORMAN DOUGLAS

Unless they behave like a bunch of professionals rather than a bunch of flinty hearted bankers, bar associations are not worthy of legal protection. They can't continue to spell 'justice' 'just us.'

MICHAEL TIGAR

There are in nature certain foundations of justice, whence all civil laws are derived but as streams.

FRANCIS BACON

Justice is a machine that, when someone has once given it the starting push, rolls on of itself.

JOHN GALSWORTHY

While the cardinal principles of justice are immutable, the methods by which justice is administered are subject to constant fluctuations.

U. S. SUPREME COURT OPINION

What we call Justice is but the organization of our egoism, which would be more noxious if it were not cabined and confined.

COUNT MAURICE MAETERLINCK

Justice is what we get when the decision is in our favor.
JOHN W. RAPER

Justice, I think, is the tolerable accommodation of the conflicting interests of society, and I don't believe there is any royal hand to attain such accommodations concretely.
LEARNED HAND

Nothing can be right and balanced again until justice is won — the injured party has to have justice. Do you understand that? Nothing can be right, for years, for lifetimes, until that first crime is punished. Or else we'd all be animals.
JOYCE CAROL OATES

Justice consists in seeing that no harm is done to men. Whenever a man cries inwardly, "Why am I being hurt?," harm is being done to him. He is often mistaken when he tries to define the harm and why and by whom it is being inflicted on him. But the cry itself is infallible.
SIMONE WEIL

Justice cannot be for one side alone, but must be for both.
ELEANOR ROOSEVELT

Justice is truth in action.
BENJAMIN DISRAELI

Justice is something that man knows little about. He may know something about charity and understanding and mercy, and he should cling to these as far as he can.
CLARENCE DARROW

Charity is no substitute for justice withheld.
ST. AUGUSTINE

Thwackum was for doing justice, and leaving mercy to heaven.
HENRY FIELDING

Blood is thicker than justice.
LOUIS NIZER

Justice and goodwill will outlast passion.
JAMES A. GARFIELD

If we had less morality we might have more justice.
DICK FRANCIS

It is the spirit and not the form of law that keeps justice alive.
EARL WARREN

I'm armed with more than complete
steel.
The justice of my quarrel.
CHRISTOPHER MARLOWE

Justice has nothing to do with expediency. It has nothing to do with any temporary standard whatever. It is rooted and grounded in the fundamental instincts of humanity.
WOODROW WILSON

Convenience and justice are often not on speaking terms.
LORD JUSTICE ACKNER

I would remind you that extremism in the defense of liberty is no vice. And let me remind you also that moderation in the pursuit of justice is no virtue.
BARRY GOLDWATER

Law and Order is like patriotism — anyone who comes on strong about patriotism has something to hide; it never fails. They always turn out to be a crook or an asshole or a traitor or something.
BILL MAULDIN

Justice, though due to the accused, is due to the accuser also.
BENJAMIN N. CARDOZO

Justice means a man's hope should not be limited by the color of his skin.
LYNDON JOHNSON

There is no such thing as justice — in or out of court.
CLARENCE DARROW

I have said to my brethren many times that I hate justice, which means that I know if a man begins to talk about that, for one reason or another he is shirking thinking in legal terms.
OLIVER WENDELL HOLMES, JR.

Justice can never be done in the midst of injustice.
SIMONE DE BEAUVOIR

Injustice is relatively easy to bear; what stings is justice.
H. L. MENCKEN

There is a point beyond which even justice becomes unjust.
SOPHOCLES

Man's capacity for justice makes democracy possible, but man's inclination to injustice makes democracy necessary.
REINHOLD NIEBUHR

Mankind censure injustice, fearing that they may be the victims of it and not because they shrink from committing it.
PLATO

It is not possible to found a lasting power upon injustice.
DEMOSTHENES

Whenever a separation is made between liberty and justice, neither, in my opinion, is safe.
EDMUND BURKE

Absolute freedom mocks at justice. Absolute justice denies freedom.
ALBERT CAMUS

No Connections, Interests, or Intercessions...will avail to prevent the strict execution of justice.
GEORGE WASHINGTON

Justice is what is established; and thus all our established laws will be regarded as just, without being examined, since they are established.

BLAISE PASCAL

Law never made men a whit more just.

HENRY DAVID THOREAU

As fashion makes what is agreeable, so it makes what is just.

BLAISE PASCAL

Be just before you're generous.

RICHARD SHERIDAN

It costs us nothing to be just.

HENRY DAVID THOREAU

A just society would be one in which liberty for one person is constrained only by the demands created by equal liberty for another.

IVAN ILLICH

The injustice to an individual is sometimes of service to the public.

JUNIUS

Every man loves justice at another man's house; nobody cares for it at his own.

PROVERB

Be just — not like man's law, which seizes on one isolated fact, but like God's judging angel, whose clear, sad eye saw all the countless cankering days of this man's life.

REBECCA HARDING DAVIS

When a just cause reaches its flood tide, as ours has done in that country, whatever stands in the way must fall before its overwhelming power.
CARRIE CHAPMAN CATT

The most certain test by which we judge whether a country is really free is the amount of security enjoyed by minorities.
LORD JOHN ACTON

The minority is always in the right.
HENRIK IBSEN

The question is simply this: Can a Negro, whose ancestors were imported into this country, and sold as slaves, become members of the political community formed and brought into existence by the Constitution of the United States, and as such become entitled to all the rights, and privileges, and immunities, guaranteed by that instrument? One of which rights is the privilege of suing in a court of the United States in cases specified by the Constitution.
ROGER B. TANEY

In respect of civil rights, common to all citizens, the Constitution of the United States does not, I think, permit any authority to know the race of those to be protected in the enjoyment of such rights.
JOHN MARSHALL HARLAN

The people can change Congress but only God can change the Supreme Court.
GEORGE W. NORRIS

Our chief justices have probably had more profound and lasting influence on their times and on the direction of the nation than most presidents have had.

RICHARD NIXON

Each of us votes independently, and I don't think a Chief Justice who tries to twist arms is going to get anywhere.

LEWIS F. POWELL, JR.

I think a Chief Justice can exercise a certain amount of leadership on the Court, but I do not think it is apt to be in a philosophical direction.

WILLIAM REHNQUIST

Marshall was not a bookish lawyer, though he was no stranger to books. He could, as wise judges do, make them his servants. He eschewed precedents such as were then available in his opinions of the Court. But he showed mastery in the treatment of precedents where they have been relied on for undesirable result.

FELIX FRANKFURTER

[John Marshall] wasn't even a lawyer.

RONALD REAGAN, *said during a 1980 Presidential debate and later rebutted by an aide who answered, "He says it wrong. That's all."*

The core of the difficulty is that there is hardly a question of any real difficulty before the Court that does not entail more than one so-called principle. Anybody can decide a question if only a single principle is in controversy.

FELIX FRANKFURTER

There is no reason to doubt that this Court may fall into error as may other branches of Government. . .The Court differs, however, from other branches of the Government in its ability to extricate itself from error. It can reconsider.

ROBERT H. JACKSON

Judges like Brandeis, Cardozo, Hughes, Murphy, Stone, and Rutledge brought to the bench a libertarian philosophy and used it to shape the law to the needs of an oncoming generation. In that sense they were "activists," criticized by many. But history will honor them for their creative work. They knew that all life is change and that law must be constantly renewed if the pressures of society are not to build up to violence and revolt.

WILLIAM O. DOUGLAS

I doubt too whether any convention we can obtain may be able to make a better Constitution; for when you assemble a number of men, to have the advantage of their joint wisdom, you inevitably assemble with those men all their prejudice, their passions, their errors of opinion, their local interests, their selfish views. From such an assembly can a perfect production be expected?

BENJAMIN FRANKLIN

That one hundred and fifty lawyers should be expected to do business together ought not to be expected.

THOMAS JEFFERSON

Our constitution does not copy the laws of neighboring states; we are rather a pattern to others than imitators ourselves. Its administration favors the many instead of the few; this is why it is called a democracy.

THUCYDIDES

As the patriots of Seventy-six did to the support of the Declaration of Independence, so to the support of the Constitution and the Laws let every American pledge his life, his property, and his sacred honor; let every man remember that to violate the law is to trample on the blood of his father, and to tear the charter of his own and his children's liberty.

ABRAHAM LINCOLN

A Constitution should be short and obscure.

NAPOLEON BONAPARTE

Our Constitution is so simple and practical that it is possible always to meet extraordinary needs by changes in emphasis and arrangement without loss of essential form.

FRANKLIN D. ROOSEVELT

Property, like liberty, though immune under the Constitution from destruction, is not immune from regulation essential for the common good. What the regulation shall be, every generation must work out itself.

BENJAMIN N. CARDOZO

The United States Constitution has proved itself the most marvelously elastic compilation of rules of government ever written.

FRANKLIN D. ROOSEVELT

I trust the friends of the proposed Constitution will never concur with its enemies, in questioning that fundamental principle of republican government which admits the right of the people to alter or abolish the established Constitution whenever they find it inconsistent with their happiness.

ALEXANDER HAMILTON

If there is any fixed star in our constitutional constellation, it is that no official, high or petty, can prescribe what shall be orthodox in politics, nationalism, religion, or other matters of opinion or force citizens to confess by word or act their faith therein.

ROBERT H. JACKSON

Praise of the Bill of Rights is proper, but we should never forget that the rights recited are fruits of the tree and not the tree itself.

ANTONIN SCALIA

If there is any principle of the Constitution that more imperatively calls for attachment than any other it is the principle of free thought — not free thought for those who agree with us but freedom for the thought we hate.

OLIVER WENDELL HOLMES, JR.

That books, newspapers, and magazines are published and sold for profit does not prevent them from being a form of expression whose liberty is safeguarded by the first Amendment. We fail to see why operation for profit should have any different effect in the case of motion pictures.

TOM C. CLARK

The First Amendment has erected a wall between church and state. That wall must be kept high and impregnable. We could not approve the slightest breach.

HUGO L. BLACK

The Fifth Amendment is an old friend and a good friend. It is one of the great landmarks in man's struggle to be free of tyranny, to be decent and civilized. It is our way to escape from the use of torture.

WILLIAM O. DOUGLAS

There is a higher law than the Constitution.

WILLIAM H. SEWARD

Our Constitution is in actual operation; everything appears to promise that it will last; but nothing in this world is certain but death and taxes.

BENJAMIN FRANKLIN

The Constitution does not forbid a third term but the unwritten law does.

ULYSSES S. GRANT

The illegal we do immediately. The unconstitutional takes a little longer.

HENRY KISSINGER

We are under a Constitution, but the Constitution is what the judges say it is.

CHARLES EVANS HUGHES

I cannot believe that a republic could subsist at the present time if the influence of lawyers in public business did not increase in proportion to the power of the people.

ALEXIS DE TOCQUEVILLE

I was well on the way to forming my present attitude toward politics as it is practiced in the United States; it is a beautiful fraud which has been imposed on the people for years, whose practitioners exchange gilded promises for the most valuable things their victims own, their votes. And who benefits most? The lawyers.

SHIRLEY CHISHOLM

The trouble with law and government is lawyers.

CLARENCE DARROW

95

The government of the United States has been emphatically termed a government of laws, and not of men. It will certainly cease to deserve this high appellation, if the laws furnish no remedy for the violation of a vested legal right.
JOHN MARSHALL

Government can easily exist without laws, but law cannot exist without government.
BERTRAND RUSSELL

In every government, though terrors reign,
Though tyrant kings or tyrant laws restrain,
How small of all that human hearts endure,
That part which laws or kings can cause or cure!
OLIVER GOLDSMITH

The best governments rest on the people, and not on the few, on persons and not on property, on the free development of public opinion and not on authority.
GEORGE BANCROFT

Why should freedom of speech and freedom of the press be allowed? Why should a government which is doing what it believes is right allow itself to be criticized? It would not allow opposition by lethal weapons. Ideas are much more fatal things than guns.
VLADIMIR I. LENIN

No law is stronger than the public sentiment where it is to be enforced. Free speech and discussion, and immunity from whip and tar and feathers, seem implied by the guarantee to each state of a "republican form of government."
ABRAHAM LINCOLN

Like the course of the heavenly bodies, harmony in national life is a resultant of the struggle between contending forces. In frank expression of conflicting opinion lies the greatest promise of wisdom in governmental action, and in suppression lies ordinarily the greatest peril.

LOUIS BRANDEIS

Justice is the end of government, it is the end of civil society. It has ever been and ever will be pursued, until it either will be obtained or until liberty be lost in the pursuit.

ALEXIS DE TOCQUEVILLE

Indeed, I tremble for my country when I reflect that God is just.

THOMAS JEFFERSON

Our government is the potent, the omnipresent teacher. For good or ill, it teaches the whole people by its example. Crime is contagious. If the Government becomes the lawbreaker, it breeds contempt for law, it invites every man to become a law unto himself, it invites anarchy.

LOUIS BRANDEIS

It was never assumed in the United States that the citizen of a free country has a right to do whatever he pleases; on the contrary, social obligations were there imposed upon him more various than anywhere else. No idea was ever entertained of attacking the principles, or of contesting the rights of society; but the exercise of its authority was divided, to the end that the office might be powerful and the officer insignificant, and that the community should be at once regulated and free. In no country in the world does the last hold so absolute a language as in America; and in no country is the right of applying it vested in so many hands.

ALEXIS DE TOCQUEVILLE

Another group in the Senate were the self-conscious law-yers, distinguished by their disposition in debate or argu-ment to preface their remarks with "speaking as a lawyer" or "thinking as a lawyer" as though this condition adds special weight to what they might say.

EUGENE MCCARTHY

The tendency of all strong Governments has always been to suppress liberty, partly in order to ease the process of rule, partly from sheer disbelief in innovation.

JOHN A. HOBSON

Experience should teach us to be most on our guard to protect liberty when the government's purposes are beneficent. Men born to freedom are naturally alert to repel invasion of their liberty by evil-minded rulers. The greatest dangers to liberty lurk in insidious encroachment by men of zeal, well-meaning but without understanding.

LOUIS BRANDEIS

Every form of bigotry can be found in ample supply in the legal system of our country. It would seem that Justice (usually depicted as a woman) is indeed blind to racism, sexism, war and poverty.

FLORYNCE R. KENNEDY

A people who proclaim their civil liberties but extend them only to a preferred group start down the path of totalitarian-ism. They emulate either the dictatorship of the Right or the dictatorship of the Left. In doing this they erase a basic distinction between our system of government and totali-tarianism.

WILLIAM O. DOUGLAS

A Government to perform even a minimum of service to its people, must take steps to suppress avarice, to strike down privately built up schemes of economic exploitation or oppression, to uproot privilege, and to assure justice and economic opportunity to the masses.

ROBERT H. JACKSON

What I am interested in is having the government of the United States more concerned about human rights than about property rights. Property is an instrument of humanity, humanity isn't an instrument of property.

WOODROW WILSON

The moment the idea is admitted into society that property is not as sacred as the laws of God, and there is not a force of law and public justice to protect it, anarchy and tyranny commence.

JOHN ADAMS

I would like to see an international court established in which to settle disputes between nations, so that armies could be disbanded and the great navies allowed to rust and rot in perfect peace.

ROBERT G. INGERSOLL

Just when I thought there was no way to stop the Japanese from steadily widening their lead over American industry, I saw a headline that said JAPAN TO OPEN ITS DOORS TO AMERICAN LAWYERS. That ought to do it.

CALVIN TRILLIN

You will see that international law is revolutionized by putting morals into it.
WOODROW WILSON

The English laws punish vice: the Chinese laws do more, they reward virtue.

OLIVER GOLDSMITH

The Law of England is a very strange one: it cannot compel anyone to tell the truth; but what it can do is give you seven years for not telling the truth.

CHARLES J. DARLING

That the king can do no wrong is a necessary and fundamental principle of the English constitution.

SIR WILLIAM BLACKSTONE

Marriage is nothing but a civil contract.

JOHN SELDEN

Marriage to many people appears to be nothing but a necessary preliminary step towards being divorced.

CHARLES J. DARLING

Matrimony and murder both carry a mandatory life sentence.

JOHN MORTIMER

Alimony — The ransom that the happy pay to the devil.

H.L. MENCKEN

Alimony is like buying oats for a dead horse.

ARTHUR "BUGS" BAER

Everybody says they'll marry till death, and they're divorced a few weeks later. I've lied to the judge twice myself.

MUHAMMAD ALI

She cried — and the judge wiped her tears with my checkbook.

> TOMMY MANVILLE, *Millionaire divorced thirteen times.*

I never hated a man enough to give him his diamonds back.

> ZSA ZSA GABOR

Judges, as a class, display, in the matter of arranging alimony, that reckless generosity which is found only in men who are giving away someone else's cash.

> P. G. WODEHOUSE

A lawyer is never entirely comfortable with a friendly divorce, any more than a good mortician wants to finish the job and then have the patient sit up on the table.

> JEAN KERR

We've got too many doctors who put personal wealth ahead of public health, too many lawyers who are more concerned with judgeships than justice.

> JESSE JACKSON

Lawyers and physicians are an ill provision for any country.

> MICHEL DE MONTAIGNE

When I am sick, then I believe in law.

> ANNA WICKHAM

Deceive not thy physician, confessor, nor lawyer.

> GEORGE HERBERT

It is hard to say whether the doctors of law or divinity have made the greater advances in the lucrative business of mystery.

EDMUND BURKE

A man must not think he can save himself the trouble of being a sensible man and gentleman by going to his lawyer, any more than he can get himself a sound constitution by going to his doctor.

EDGAR HOWE

I leave this rule for others when I'm
   dead,
Be always sure you're right — then go
   ahead.

DAVY CROCKETT

Why is there always a sacred singing
When a lawyer cashes in?
Why does a hearse horse snicker
Hauling a lawyer away?

CARL SANDBURG

Why may not that be the skull of a lawyer? Where be his quidities now, his quillets, his cases, his tenures, and his tricks?

WILLIAM SHAKESPEARE,
Hamlet

When you have told anyone you have left him a legacy the only decent thing to do is to die at once.
SAMUEL BUTLER

So, my judges, face death with a good hope, and know for certain that no evil can happen to a good man, either in life or after death.
SOCRATES

Why, gentlemen, you cannot live without lawyers, and certainly you cannot die without them.
JOSEPH CHOATE

Don't worry, I'm going to outlive those bastards.
THURGOOD MARSHALL

INDEX OF AUTHORS